THE
Archive Photographs
SERIES
AROUND
STOCKSBRIDGE
THE SECOND SELECTION

We dedicate this book to the late Fred and Mary Hepworth who played an active part in the running of Stocksbridge & District History Society and did much to promote interest in all things historical in the valley. Both Mary and Fred had a keen interest in antiques, books, community life, the environment and much, much more, being members of many groups and societies.

Fred was born in Stocksbridge and spent most of his working life in the steel works. He was particularly interested in the history of early man. He discovered the Mesolithic (Middle Stone Age) site at Deepcar in 1948, helped in its excavation and recording in 1962 and unveiled the commemorative stone placed at the site on 13 October 1995.

Mary would jokingly refer to herself as an 'incomer', despite having lived in Stocksbridge for over 50 years! She was the treasurer of the History Society for many years, was extremely knowledgeable about the area and made valuable contributions to several books written about the locality, including our first *Around Stocksbridge* book of photographs.

It is due to people like Mary and Fred, who valued their heritage and committed it to print, that books such as this can be compiled. Long may these publications continue!

THE
Archive Photographs
SERIES
AROUND
STOCKSBRIDGE
THE SECOND SELECTION

Compiled by
Brenda Duffield
Basil Spooner
Christine Herbert
of the
Stocksbridge & District History Society

TEMPUS

First published 1998
Copyright © Stocksbridge & District History Society, 1998

Tempus Publishing Limited
The Mill, Brimscombe Port,
Stroud, Gloucestershire, GL5 2QG

ISBN 0 7524 1163 2

Typesetting and origination by
Tempus Publishing Limited
Printed in Great Britain by
Midway Clark Printing, Wiltshire

'Cat and Dog Life at Stocksbridge'. This postcard was produced from a photograph taken by local photographer, William Beckett. The two animals were *Spot* and *Suzie*, the family pets of the Smith family who lived at Bank View, Hole House Lane, Stocksbridge.

Contents

This map is taken from Bacon's *County Map of Yorkshire, c.* 1910. The colours of the original map distinguish between administrative boundaries. Hordron, Langsett and Midhopestones were included in Penistone Rural District, while all land south of the Little Don River, including Bradfield, lay in Wortley Rural District. Stocksbridge Urban District, comprising Bolsterstone Parish, further included Hunshelf and Greenmoor. The population of Stocksbridge Urban District was given as 6,566. Note the misspelling of Walder's Hill.

Introduction

A handbook for ramblers entitled *Twelve Rambles Near Sheffield*, compiled from a series of articles appearing in the *Sheffield Daily Independent* in the early 1900s, begins with Deepcar to Bamford;

'The route lies along the edge of the great open moorland that divides the upper courses of the Don and the Derwent, and is perhaps the most romantic in the whole of the Sheffield region, if both natural beauty and historical suggestion are appreciated.

The railway journey to Deepcar through the Wharncliffe Woods enables us to imagine what much of the valley scenery round Sheffield once was like. There was an abundance of unenclosed forest. The western side of the Don Valley, which runs up eventually to Onesmoor, is bitten out into several little lateral valleys that come to a dead end. The third valley opening is the Ewden, which cuts right through up to the untenanted moors.

Just before reaching Deepcar the Wharncliffe rocks, on which neck-endangering climbers practise, appear high up on the right, across a fire-scarred clearance of wood.

Deepcar, at the junction of the Don and the Little Don, seems to be an entirely modern place - a product of industrialism.'

Pause here for gasps of indignation and disbelief, then consider how it must have appeared to a visitor, ignorant of the long history of Deepcar. Little did he know that he had passed a Mesolithic site on his walk down Station Road. He carries on over the Don, into the Wortley road, over the Little Don, across the Sheffield to Langsett high road opposite the King and Miller and up past the school.

'There is a rise of 600 feet from Deepcar to the top of Bolsterstone Common, and wise walkers will begin steadily…the first half hour breaks the back of the day's task by placing you a thousand feet high [above sea level]. The scenery has no distinction at present. The bare slopes of the Stocksbridge valley, or Midhope Dale as it was once called, are not attractive. The interest of the ascent is in the gannister and coal shafts that abound, rather than in the scenery. The stone in the quarry you pass has a coaly look. Formally you could walk into a coal pit in the hillside hereabout.

The approach to Bolsterstone is dramatic. It is the most compactly grouped, clean little village that you ever saw… It stands complete on the flat of the hilltop. You have been toiling up the hill with nothing more interesting to see than a disused mine shaft - a mere deserted pulley-wheel and scanty bank of refuse - when half a dozen steps bring the village suddenly into full view. The church, the school, the open village space - no longer green - the vicarage, the little inn, all cluster with no trace of straggling. The impression the place produces on the mind is always pleasing, for it contrasts the sweetness of the agricultural high lands with the dinginess of the industrial valleys.'

We cannot argue with this last impression when we take into account the cost to the environment of the industrialisation, which brought more material prosperity to the depressed agricultural areas like Bolsterstone Parish during the 'hungry forties'. Having said that, we can also appreciate the pleasure derived by our anonymous rambler from a journey that has been travelled by many over the years and we rejoice that the village has been maintained as completely as it has.

The present volume of photographs begins in a similar vein, with excursions to the beauty spots surrounding our town - Bolsterstone, Ewden Valley, Langsett, Midhope and Wortley - which will remain as sources of pleasure and inspiration into the twenty-first century. We also pay tribute to the hardy souls, life-long villagers and newcomers alike, who worked hard and played hard.

In the days of large families it seems that those in trade, who were able to take advantage of the growing market for consumer goods, at last achieved some measure of prosperity. Another yardstick of progress was the technical advance of motorised transport, a vital element in the industrial growth of our valley.

We cannot ignore the interruptions in progress which occurred in 1914 and 1939, when so many of our young men and women went to serve their country, some never to return. Some had the time of their lives, while others returned but were never the same again.

B. Duffield
1998

Acknowledgements

We would like to thank the following people for lending us their prized photographs: P. Barr, J.M. Clark, J. Clegg, T. Cooke, J.T. Copley, B. Fidler, S. Fieldsend, Frith's Postcards, J. Gibson, F. Harrison, K. Hepworth, A. Herbert, B. Hodgkinson, T. Hoyle, J. Hudson, M. Hull, F. Jennings, W. Kaye, E.M. Lindley, M. Lindley, G. Mansell, J. Marsden, A.A. McKay, B. Mckay, E.M. McKinlay, N. Mozley, Old Barnsley Photographs, J. Oxspring, N. Pears, N. Pickering, J. Plusa, A. Sampson, Stocksbridge Archive, C. Suggett, M. Todner, J. Walton, M. Wilson, S. Woodcock. We would also like to thank all those who have helped with research. The photographs of Langsett navvy huts and Ewden are reproduced by permission of Yorkshire Water plc. A number of photographs have been developed from negatives lent to us by the grandson of Denis Leather, who took them in the 1930s. We are further grateful to B. Fidler of Chapeltown, onetime Police Officer at Deepcar police station, for lending us *The Ramblers' Handbook*. We are grateful for the photographic work contributed by A.A. McKay and Trevor Lodge and are indebted to H.O. Duffield for his support and help in the preparation of this publication.

Part I : Excursions

One
Westward to Langsett

Our journey around Stocksbridge begins at St Matthias Church, which opened on 1 November 1890. To the right of the church is Rimington Row. This row of houses has since been demolished. They were originally back-to-back houses with the roadside properties used as shops. The property on the extreme right has been in the Hepworth family for many years and was latterly owned by the late Mary and Fred Hepworth, to whom this book is dedicated.

Travelling west along Manchester Road, we find ourselves outside the premises of M. Blackburn, milliner. Next door stands the Coach and Horses public house where, in 1842, Samuel Fox met Denton at 'Willie Jubb's'. The next building, along the snow covered street, is that of the Miners Welfare Works Institute, built in 1910. Its function was 'to promote useful knowledge, social intercourse and recreation of an innocent and improving character'. Available to members, for the sum of 2/6d per half year, were a reading room, a play room, billiards, a smoke room, refreshments and entertainment. It was open every day except Sunday. The president was W.H. Fox, the secretary was Edward Bramley.

Despite the smoking chimneys and factory buildings, we can see here just how rural Stocksbridge was in the early years of this century. Brownhill Row can be clearly seen slanting diagonally up the Hunshelf Bank hillside. The terrace in the right foreground is Hope Street, which remains as residential property today. Ironically the end-on terraces of Johnson Street, in the centre of the picture, cited by Dr Robertshaw, in 1927, as being the least healthy street in the area, now form the site of the Health Centre and car parks.

Here we are looking down Pearson Street, where many workers were housed in the late nineteenth century. The number of households at Horner House in 1851 was only seven, this had risen to sixty-three by the time of the 1881 census. Many of the additional families came from Bradwell in Derbyshire, the home of Samuel Fox. These houses were valued at £100 in 1869. The photograph dates either from the 1904 celebration of the founding of the local branch of the Salvation Army or from the 1919 peace celebrations. The building on the left was used as a branch of the West Riding public library until the 1940s.

Across from Pearson Street stood Horner House Farm, which is now the site of a residential home for the elderly. The terraces seen here are Langsett Terrace and Webb Terrace. The former is dwarfed by the Siemen's building and the chimneys of Samuel Fox's works. The date is c. 1968, just prior to the demolition of the farm. The date stone from the farm, which reads 1662, was saved and placed in a nearby wall.

Further west along Manchester Road is the area known as Hawthorn Brook. The source of the brook is probably one of the numerous springs which rise from the hillside behind the houses seen on the right of the picture. The houses on the right, with the 'donkey-stoned' steps, no longer exist.

Pictured here is Unsliven Bridge and the channel leading from Underbank Reservoir, *c.* 1906. Note the misspelling of Unsleven, a word said to have derived from unshriven, meaning unblessed. Another possibility, according to Joseph Kenworthy, is that the name is a corruption of Hunshelf. The earliest mention of this area was in 1450. In 1601 John Greaves of Windhill bequeathed 3/4d, 'toward the making of Unshriven Brigge, whensoever it shall be made'.

By following Unsliven Road we come to Langley Brook Farm. This farm dates back for many years, records show that in 1661 a tenant by the name of John Cauldwell died here. In 1702 the occupant was Jonathan Hadfield who was Deputy Constable of Bradfield. Generations of the Crawshaw family inhabited the farm between 1841 and 1881. A public right of way to Midhope runs through the farmyard. Apparently Langley Brook ceased to be a working farm following an outbreak of foot and mouth disease in the mid-1930s.

Damstakes Farm, once the home of the Barden family, was the next property on the journey to Midhope. The site of the farm now lies under the waters of Underbank Reservoir!

This view looks west along Manchester Road towards Midhope crossroads. The village bobby, possibly 'Bobby' Mate, is out for a stroll with two well dressed ladies. The building on the left is the house of Dawson the wheelwright, the one on the right is Lower Hand Bank Farm, formerly the Rose and Crown. The latter is of the same design as both the Waggon and Horses, at Langsett, and Sheephouse Farm. They were all built by William Payne who bought the Manor of Langsett in 1803.

Midhope Hall Farm. This was built on the site of the ancient Midhope Hall. The barn was built on the site of the Court House. The original lines of the dungeon walls and the timber bar, where the prisoners stood, were charted with the help of Horace Uttley, a dowser who could find metal or bodies using hazel twigs. He undertook work for the police and the water board.

Milnes' Cottage, sometimes referred to as the White House, for obvious reasons, can be seen here in Lower Midhope. The left part of the cottage was at one time used as a chapel. Joshua Milnes was born here in 1844. He started work at Fox's aged 10 and walked there and back each day. He finally retired in 1922 after 67 years service! Note the 'causey' and sunken road surface.

Uskers, or Huskers, Farm lies at the bottom of Langsett Hill. It formed part of the Underbank Estate belonging to William Fenton. The farm was tenanted by Herbert Marsden in 1899, at which time Barnsley Corporation Water appropriated 11 of the 32 acres of land. Leonard Hill occupied the farm in the 1920s, his daughter Marjorie can be seen standing in the doorway. The sign to the front of the farm reads The Cyclist's Touring Club.

Continuing up the road towards Langsett village, in 1905, we would have passed these navvy huts which housed the construction workers, along with their families, who were employed to built Langsett Reservoir. (Photograph courtesy of Sheffield Library.)

Across the road and sited just below the Waggon and Horses public house, which can just be seen on the extreme right of the picture, stood the canteen and workmen's café, providing facilities for the construction workers.

In 1910 we can see that, lying to the rear of the canteen, in full view of the newly constructed Langsett dam wall, was Langsett Park. The site is presently occupied by some of the filter beds and treatment works.

Here we see Langsett village with Stanley House on the right, the White House in the centre and, on the left, the Waggon and Horses' old harness room.

Langsett House. The house was tenanted by the Bradleys until 1896, when Sheffield Corporation Water appropriated extensive lands in both the Penistone and Ecclesfield parishes. The property is currently partly residential and partly used as a visitor centre.

'The Langsett Lads', photographed at Upper Midhope. Standing is Ira Lawton and perched on the gate, second from the left, is Benny Windle.

Two
Across the Bridge and Eastwards

Stocksbridge Town Hall and Church.

Our second excursion starts at the Town Hall. This was built after 1912 when Stocksbridge Urban District Council bought the site of the old council offices from Samuel Fox on the expiration of the lease. It was built by David Brearley and Sons and opened in 1928. In later years the wall-mounted post box was replaced by a pillar box, the lamps on the corners of the building were removed when street lighting was improved and a pedestrian crossing was added. The road which falls away to the left of the picture is Hunshelf Road, locally known as Smithy Hill, which heads towards the river and the works. (Photograph courtesy of Sheffield Library.)

This is the site of the original Stocks Bridge that gave rise to the name of the town. There is still some debate as to whether the bridge was named after Mr Stocks, who owned the land, or after the fulling stocks belonging to the nearby cotton mill. The original bridge was a footbridge with a ford alongside. This was replaced by a carriage bridge, erected in 1812 and paid for by a consortium. The three-storey building on the left has been used as a shop for most of its existence. In 1881 it was John Milnes' grocer and draper's shop, later it was owned by the Rushbys and it is currently owned by the Hanwells. The terrace immediately above the shop is Gentleman's Row, which was the superior housing used to accommodate the foremen in Fox's. The row of houses in the right foreground is Bath Terrace.

A later view of the same area shows Bank House in the centre foreground. This was once a doctor's surgery, run by Dr Mossman and then later by Dr Goldie. More recently, prior to its demolition, it was used as the work's drawing office. With the introduction of the Stocksbridge railway - the rails run across the foreground of the picture - the building to the right of Bank House was erected to serve as the Railway Dining Rooms. Wedding receptions were often held here. The other terraces on the hillside are Honeymoon Row (centre) and Derbyshire Row (right). (Photograph courtesy of Sheffield Library.)

After crossing the bridge, we turn right along Ford Lane and pass by Bath Terrace, named after the Bath House which stood nearby. Samuel Fox built a lot of housing for his workers, mostly rows of terraced housing, such as this. The Ollerenshaws at one time lived in the first house from the left.

Bath Terrace once again, this time at a 1945 Victory party. The families living there at this time were those of Marsden, Marsh, Sanderson, Day, Watkinson, Beever, Coney and Harrison. The row looked out on the old Bath House and the Japan Shop, which belonged to the works.

This is a view outside Moonpenny Farm on Ford Lane, *c.* 1914. Showing off their new calf, Daisy, are, from left to right, Pat Birch, Billy Nixon (on the stool), Fred Wood and Fred Rodgers. This area is now a car park.

Scotch Row is the name given to the houses in the immediate foreground. The name was derived from the method of construction rather than the origin of their occupants. These were back-to-back houses, their occupants in 1891 being the families of Ashforth, Birch, Sharpe, Briggs, Wilson, Ramsden, Gillott, Naylor, Liles, Jackson and Day. Joseph Jackson of 124 Scotch Row was, in 1909, the Secretary of Sheffield Equalised Independent Druids, Stocksbridge Branch. The lodge had 428 members and met at the Congregational School. (Photograph courtesy of Sheffield Library.)

The houses of Wood Willows, now 356 to 378 Manchester Road, are on the boundary between Stocksbridge and Deepcar. The properties were built before 1908. Fox's stainless department was later built behind them. The walls of these houses are so thick that on the night of the Sheffield Blitz at least one family was not even aware that there was a raid on! At that time the bathrooms were in the cellar, with natural light entering through a skylight in the backyard.

Henholmes Bridge, at the Deepcar end of Ford Lane, looks more like our idea of the original Stocks Bridge. It was erected by the Turners, who owned the nearby pipeworks. The pipeworks were later taken over by J. Armitage. Prior to the bridge being built there was only a ford here. The house just over the bridge was known as the Gatehouse and was owned by Fox's. The occupant (at one time Coney and later Walton) had to man the level-crossing gates where the railway and access road crossed. The three-storey house to the left of the picture was once the home of C. Hinchliffe of Wharncliffe Press, who was responsible for the printing of *Hinchliffe's Stocksbridge Almanack* in the early 1900s. His printer's workshop was situated in the lower rooms of the house.

The area known as Old Heywoods, in Deepcar, is a linear development eastwards along Manchester Road. Being built on a hillside, the houses have three storeys to the rear. It was not unusual for the houses to be divided and sub-let; one family to the front, one to the back. The houses were built in the latter part of the nineteenth century. Only nine households were registered in this area in the 1851 census. (Photograph courtesy of Sheffield Library.)

Woodbine Villas, Deepcar, c. 1910. The only record of this property being named Woodbine Villas is the inscription on this card! The house at the far end of the row has always been known locally as The Water House. The house was built by Mr Brearley in 1897 for his own use and was subsequently bought by the Sheffield Corporation Waterworks. There was an office at the back where people would pay their water rates. (Photograph courtesy of Sheffield Library.)

Three
Up the Don to Wortley

Deepcar crossroads, *c.* 1905. From the old, wooden, three-fingered signpost we look down Vaughton Hill. This was named after the family who kept the ale-house which became known as the Travellers' Inn. It was known locally as the Low Drop because it was the lowest of the three properties on the slope. The tall chimneys in the background were part of Lowood's Refractories. The railway bridge, carrying trains from Samuel Fox's to Wortley and beyond, can be seen on the left of the picture. (Photograph courtesy of Sheffield Library.)

The Florence Buildings in Deepcar were known locally as Donkey View. They were back-to-back houses built to house the workers at Armitage's brick works. They were named after John Armitage's wife. The houses were built between the river and the brick works. The railway bridge from Fox's can be seen in the background. (Photograph courtesy of Sheffield Library.)

Having passed under the railway bridge (just visible among the trees on the left), we proceed towards Soughley bridge, turning to look back towards a 1915 view of Deepcar. The spoil heaps, which flanked the Deepcar to Wortley road, are clearly visible. These smouldered and burned for decades before they were cleared to make way for the building of the Stocksbridge bypass.

On the way to Wortley a short detour to the left takes us to see the, much photographed, beauty spot near the Tin Mill, called the Wortley Leppings. The old wooden bridge, seen here in 1910, has long since gone and has been replaced by a metal one. The 'Leppings', however, still remain and are passable with care.

St Leonard's church, Wortley, was founded during the reign of Henry III in the thirteenth century. The square tower is the oldest part of the building and the eight bells were cast in 1893. The main door into the church was made by the firm of Robert Thompson, of Kilburn in North Yorkshire. He was more famously known as the 'mouseman' as he carved a mouse trademark on each piece of furniture that he made.

The Lych Gate, Wortley, near Sheffield.

Wortley church has two lychgates. The northern one is a memorial to those killed in the First World War. The eastern lychgate (seen above) bears carvings of alpha and omega, symbolising the beginning and the end, on the base stones. In the centre of the gateway is the stone on which coffin bearers would rest their burden.

Wortley Hall. Lords of the Manor of Wortley can be traced back to the twelfth century. The hall has been rebuilt several times since then. The most famous occupant of the hall was probably Sir Francis Wortley I, who fought for King Charles I in the Civil War and was imprisoned in the Tower of London for his exploits. The present building was begun in the eighteenth century. During the Second World War the Hall was occupied by the army.

Four
Down the Bitholmes to Morehall

Our starting point for this excursion is Mangle Row, in Deepcar, seen here c. 1924. This property stood on Manchester Road opposite Vaughton Hill. Its name derives from the communal mangle, which stood at the top of the central 'gennel' or passageway. The family standing nearest to the camera is the Green family, in the middle are the Emerson brothers and their wives and farthest away are the Fieldsend family. Other occupants of the row included the Clark and Eustace families.

Heading east from Deepcar, the valley is overshadowed by the presence of Wharncliffe Crags. This was the venue for many an outing or picnic in the days before the motor car made trips further afield more accessible. This 1904 view shows the sliding stone where many trouser seats would have been worn through by the coarse gritstone. The Edwardian lady, seen here having a slide, looks rather incongruous in her long skirts!

The waterfall on Wharncliffe Crags is located below Dragon's Well, near the Dragon's Den or Cave. It would have been forbidden territory for these young boys when it formed part of the Wharncliffe Chase.

The route out of Deepcar takes us along the Bitholmes towards Morehall. The word Bitholmes is said to have derived from 'by the holmes', holmes being the word for a flat flood plain. It is hard to imagine this area ever having been a flat flood plain as the River Don is now many feet below road level. The road passes through one of the few remaining areas of ancient woodland to be found locally, which, in Spring, is covered by a mass of bluebells. (Photograph courtesy of Sheffield Library.)

More Hall itself dates from before 1100. There would almost certainly have been a farm there, from this time, in order to provide food for the occupants of the 'big house'. The farm buildings, seen in the centre of the present farm, certainly date back to the mid-seventeenth century, as Bolsterstone glass was used for the windows. The barn on the extreme left can be traced back even earlier as it was constructed on crucks, the timbers probably date from the mid-sixteenth century. It became the property of Lord Wharncliffe in 1862 and Joseph Sheldon wrote about living and working there in the 1860s for Joseph Crossland.

As we make our way up the steep hill, we pass Carr Lane Top. In 1851 one of the cottages was occupied by William Shaw, a mole catcher, along with his wife and seven children. By 1881 his son, Aaron, occupied one of the cottages with his family. He worked in a stone quarry while two of his sons, aged 12 and 13, were coal mine 'hurriers'. His sister Annice lived in another of the cottages with her husband, George Senior, an umbrella-rib hardener for Fox's. George Wragg, a quarryman, occupied the third cottage and John Brearley, a stonemason, occupied the fourth.

Nearing Bolsterstone, we see Broom Cottage on the left of Morehall Lane. This cottage was built after 1851. In 1881 it was occupied by John Whiteley. It was later occupied by Wallace Charlesworth, grandfather of Fred Hepworth.

Five
Up 'The Route' to Ewden

EWDEN VALLEY, SHEFFIELD

This view shows the Ewden Valley prior to the construction of More Hall Reservoir. The building of the dam began in 1913 but the onset of the First World War delayed its completion. It was officially opened in 1929. This excursion takes us along the Ewden Valley, through Ewden Village and then westwards, along the south side of Broomhead Reservoir.

Dwarriden dates back many centuries. One owner of the property, Henry Hawkesworth of Dwaryden, must have been a wealthy man. When he died, c. 1686, he left the following to his grandson Thomas, 'furniture from the dwelling-house, plough, harrow, whaine, yokes and teame, joyner tools and fowling piece.' Rooms mentioned in the inventory include: the house, great parlour, little parlour, chamber over the parlour, chamber over the house and a buttery. Animals included 1 swine, 4 oxen, 5 cows, 2 bullocks, 1 calf, 3 horses and sheep.

A close up of the date stone, seen over the door in the previous picture, indicates that Thomas used some of his new found wealth to rebuild or remodel the property.

"Old Wigtwizzle"

We travel away from Broomhead Reservoir to the, one-time, hamlet of Wigtwizzle. Old Wigtwizzle, or Wigtwizzle Farm, was the home farm of Wigtwizzle Hall. It was tenanted by the family of Thompson in the eighteenth century. It was demolished, before the hall, early in the twentieth century.

Heading back towards Bolsterstone we would have passed Broomhead Mill House, the site of which now lies under the waters of Broomhead Reservoir. This was a licensed public house until George Staniforth, of Bolsterstone, was killed on the premises, *c.* 1855, as the result of an argument over a dog fight. The licence was rescinded by Mr James Rimington Wilson, after which the building was demolished to be replaced by the one seen above.

New Mill Bridge was a packhorse bridge and was actually 'new' in the thirteenth century! It stood over Ewden Beck, near Ewden Village. It was removed, stone by stone, prior to the reservoir being filled and was then rebuilt in Glen Howe Park, Wharncliffe Side, where it can still be seen today. The timber building was one of the Waterwork's houses and was among the first residences in the area to boast a bathroom.

As we make our way back up the hill to Bolsterstone, we pass Yew Trees Farm. In 1851 the curate of Bolsterstone, John Bell, lodged at the seventy-acre farm, which was run by the Newton family. Census returns show that the Newton family ran the farm, at intervals, for over 50 years.

Six

Bolsterstone

The panorama of Bolsterstone Village is seen here from Walder's Low cairn. The cairn was raised, by Charles Macro Wilson, in the 1870s, on the spot where the Saxon chief Walder is reputed to be buried. It stands at 1000 feet above sea level. It is on private land but can be viewed from the public footpath that skirts the nearby golf course.

The Porter's Lodge, Bolsterstone. The Rockleys, of Worsborough, founded a chapel here in 1409. On the other side of the green is the Manor House of Waldershelf, an ancient structure built, in the fashion of the church, with bow windows. In 1580/81 'named lands in Waldershelf' were conveyed, by William Rockley, to George, Earl of Shrewsbury. By 1637, half of the manor house had been let to Thomas Morton and the remaining half to John Birks and John Swinden. (Photograph courtesy of Sheffield Library.)

The Castle Inn, c. 1907. According to the sign the landlady, at this time, was Ann Bramall. The previous landlord had been her father-in-law, Thomas Henry Bramall. Ann bought the premises, together with '6 closes of land', for £4,750 in January 1907. She was the daughter of Joseph Grayson, coalmerchant, of Leeke House, Haywoods.(Photograph courtesy of Sheffield Library.)

The New Cottages were built, in the late 1920s, by George and Lawrence Lindley. They were highly commended by the Council for Preservation of Rural England for the development. The site was formerly occupied by barns and stabling belonging to Ann Bramall of the Castle Inn.

Bolsterstone Village Green, in 1938. The village pump was fenced in when people no longer needed it for their water supply. There were four other wells around the village, some of which were in daily use until relatively recent times. The hearse house was converted from a smithy, the chimney of which can still be seen. Although motor-powered vehicles can be seen near the church, horses were still used on many occasions.

The Vicarage, in Bolsterstone, was built in the 1860s. Its first occupant was the Revd William Rimington, who was succeeded by the Revd W.R. Wilson. It stands on the ridge overlooking the Ewden valley and is rather exposed to the elements. The lane running past the property leads to the aptly named Wind Hill. It comes as no surprise, therefore, to find that this was the first house in the area to be fitted with double glazing!

Traditional ploughing in Bolsterstone. Annual ploughing matches were held, alternately in Bolsterstone and Wigtwizzle, with entrants arriving from all over England. Thomas Milnes of Greave House won the first match in 1880. In 1908 the winner of the Champion Prize was Luther Morris of Hand Bank, Midhope, in 1910 it was won by Spencer Shaw. Other winners included W.H. Crawshaw of Langley Brook and George Buckley of Fairest (four times each). The Webster family of Castle Farm, Bolsterstone won many times, Arnold Webster won the last Championship, in 1938.

Seven
Back to Stocksbridge via The Glen

The final part of our excursion leads us from Bolsterstone back to the centre of Stocksbridge via The Glen, Deepcar. This delightful detour was missed by our early rambler. More commonly known as Fox Glen, this area is a small valley of land which was bestowed upon the people of Deepcar and Stocksbridge, by the trustees of the late Samuel Fox, in commemoration of the coronation of George V and Queen Mary, in 1911. The original entrance is seen here at the bottom of a narrow winding road. We believe that its demolition was effected by a runaway traction engine! The main path ran alongside the river.

Fox Glen in 1917. The steep sides of the Glen were criss-crossed with paths, some of them stepped like this one. The area was well used by families for Sunday walks and picnics in the summer. Local choirs and bands held concerts here too. (Photograph courtesy of Sheffield Library.)

Being central to both Deepcar and Stocksbridge, Fox Glen was often chosen as the venue for special events in which the whole valley was to be involved. Services were held here to mark the end of the First World War. Here we see the May Queen celebrations of 1924. The queen was Nellie Berwick.

This gun stood, pointing in the direction of Sheffield, on a mound of land to the northern side of Fox Glen, during the 1930s. Evidently it provided a focal point for young boys at play.

By the 1930s, Fox Glen had a seesaw, a sandpit, swings and a roundabout. Further up the Glen there were a series of paddling pools and a dammed area that was used, by the hardy, as a swimming pool. The concrete steps, to the right of the swings, are the only remaining part of the playground area. They have been cleaned in recent years and the area has been used as a carol concert venue.

From the western end of Fox Glen we cut through the Stubbin farmland to Bracken Moor. Bracken Moor Farm was occupied by the Kenworthy family for three generations through the early 1900s. There was a stable, hay loft and pig sties at the end of the garden, along with a tennis court. Brook Row, just below the farm, was named after the owner of the pipe and brick works. This works produced the yellow bricks from which the houses were built.

The final stretch of our journey takes us back down the hill towards the centre of Stocksbridge, passing through Bocking Wood, pictured here c. 1905. The child at the front is Dorothy Hance (née Jackson). Her father, Ernest, owned a greengrocer's business on Rimington Row, facing the wood. He was also the local Fire Chief. The area is now occupied by the Scout headquarters and the Stocksbridge cemetery.

PART II : LIFE IN STEEL VALLEY

Eight
Church Parade

This memorial to the 'Change Ringers' of 1909 can be seen in the bell tower of St Mary's church, in Bolsterstone. St Mary's was the only church in the area to have such a set of bells and a feat of this kind called for a major celebration. The descendants of the men mentioned on this memorial remain in the area to this day, many of them still having strong connections with Bolsterstone and the church.

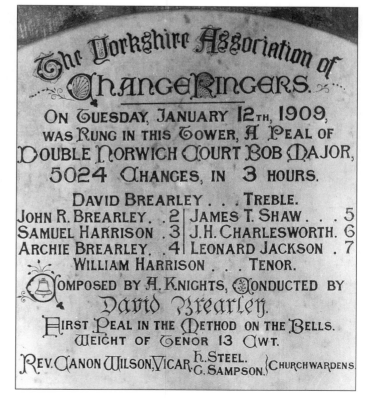

The Yorkshire Association of Change Ringers.

On Tuesday, January 12th, 1909, was Rung in this Tower, A Peal of Double Norwich Court Bob Major, 5024 Changes, in 3 Hours.

DAVID BREARLEY . . . TREBLE.
JOHN R. BREARLEY . . 2 | JAMES T. SHAW . . . 5
SAMUEL HARRISON . 3 | J. H. CHARLESWORTH. 6
ARCHIE BREARLEY . . 4 | LEONARD JACKSON . 7
WILLIAM HARRISON . . . TENOR.

Composed by A. Knights, Conducted by David Brearley.

First Peal in the Method on the Bells.
Weight of Tenor 13 Cwt.

Rev. Canon Wilson, Vicar, H. Steel. G. Sampson. Churchwardens

As with many small communities, Whitsuntide was a major event on the year's calendar. Here we see the gentlemen of the string quintet, lining up with their predominantly male entourage, outside the post office at Midhopestones in 1907. This building has recently been demolished.

Another Whitsuntide gathering, this time on Bolsterstone Green, in 1909. For such events everyone would turn out in their Sunday best, with the young girls dressed in their new summer finery, whatever the weather. They packed the public places where the the parade was scheduled to stop and sang Whitsuntide hymns accompanied by the band, here almost swamped by the throng.

The churches were often a focal point for carnivals. This is the Bolsterstone Carnival of 1923. The ladies are, from left to right: Lilley Haigh, Nellie Cooke, Mrs R. Shaw, Mrs T. Westhead, Nellie Rodgers, Mrs Dyson and Mrs Donkersley.

It wasn't just the ladies who enjoyed dressing up! Here we see the Bolsterstone Men's Group having fun. On the back row, second from the left, is 'Walshy' Gill and third from the right is Herbert Swallow. On the front row, second from the left, is George Hall.

Members of the Green Moor United Methodist Sunday School assembled outside the new Green Moor Chapel prior to the Whitsuntide procession, *c.* 1915. This chapel was built between 1910 and 1914.

The interior of the Green Moor Methodist Chapel, *c.* 1915. On the back row, from left to right, are: Herbert Ward, Douglas Wordsworth, George Wright, Edmund Bramall, Wilfred Walton (organist), -?-, George Bramall, John Wordsworth, Arthur Bramall, J. W. Maxwell, Sidney Walton, Frank Bramall, -?- and W. Smith. The ladies are, from left to right: Clara Goddard, Annie Bramall, Ginnie Beever, -?-, Miriam Hoyle, Ida Buxton, -?-, Miriam Spencely, Mary Spencely and Laura Spencely. Seated at the front are Mr Batty (left) and Mr F. Walton.

'The Deepcar Workers', poised for action in St John's church in Deepcar. The church was built in 1878 but obviously had no central heating installed at that time for the men in the picture are chiseling out holes to accommodate the pipes, which are still there today. Gas fittings were installed in the church in 1885, courtesy of Samuel Fox.

Outside the Wesley Hall, belonging to the Wesleyan Methodist Church in Manchester Road, Deepcar, we see a bible class in the early years of the century. On the back row, from left to right: Haydn Holling, Arnold Worsley, -?-, Bertie Butcher, -?-, -?-, -?-, Leonard Holling, -?-, Arthur Gabbitas. Centre row, from left to right: Charlie Johnson, Albert Hirst, Emmie Hirst, -?-, George Lindley, Tommy Faulkner, -?-, -?-, John West, -?-. Seated, from left to right: Mrs Mary Roberts, Mrs Faulkner, -?-, Mrs Leonard Holling, -?-, -?-, Mrs Ted Knowles, -?-.

The Stocksbridge Parsonage, the building of which was financed by Samuel Fox, stood at the corner of Bocking Hill and Haywood Lane. A Bolsterstone church magazine of January 1886 states that 'The house for the clergyman at Stocksbridge...is now complete and occupied by the Revd A.M. Winter.' This indicates that the parsonage pre-dates St Matthias church by some five years.

Stocksbridge became a parish in its own right in 1917. Here we see the induction of the new vicar, Revd H.C. Foster, on 8 September 1917. He had served as a navy chaplain, attached to HMS *Victory*. He served with the Royal Naval Division at Antwerp and at the Gallipoli landing. On 8 October 1917, the first wedding ceremony was performed here, the marriage of Miss Dorothy Barraclough and Mr Harvey Mitchell.

St Ann's Roman Catholic Church, in Deepcar, was opened in 1859 in the face of local opposition. The site was only secured through the actions of an individual intermediary. Funding was provided as the result of an appeal to the generosity of the people of Dublin. A note in the Diamond Jubilee souvenir programme records that a Roman Catholic Chapel had existed at Spink House, c. 1870.

The original building of 1859 was extended between 1919 and 1921, at which time the interior layout was changed. The altar now stands to the left.

The St Ann's Catholic Young Men's Society, seen here between the wars. Back row, from left to right: Jack Curran, John Conroy, Jimmy Lowry, Mr Regan, Tom Regan, Mick Mannion, Con Keogh, Tommy Moran, Aiden Staniforth, Emile Moran, Dennis Moran, Vincent Ward, Roland Jackson, Ernest Marsh and Eric Tune. Middle row, from left to right: Jack Moran, Michael Moran, Charles Sullivan, Edgar Staniforth, Michael Kelly, John Kielly, Johnny

O'Brien, John Barret, -?-, Arnold Staniforth, Leonard Staniforth, Pat O'Hagan, Bernard Green, Jimmy Dodds and John O'Hagan. Front row, from left to right: Lawrence O'Mahony, John Burke, Tommy Keogh, John Edward Tune, Bernard Mannion, Billy Jackson, Harry Lavery, Tommy Moran, Father T. Moynihan (parish priest 1925 - 1939), -?-, Joe Haley, Joseph Marsden, Henry Marsden, John Haley and Stuart ?

The Salvation Army meeting place was initially in Pearson Street, from 1904. In 1913 they began to meet in Edward Street, in the basement of a building belonging to Schofields which was then the Electric Theatre. Finally, in 1935, a purpose built Citadel, in Victoria Street, was opened by the Countess of Wharncliffe.

The Salvation Army Sunday School anniversary, in July 1953. Standing at the back, on the extreme left and right, respectively, of the photograph are Captain and Mrs Palmer. The standard bearer is C. Broadhead. In front of them, from left to right: N. Stanniland, M. Spooner, G. Cheetham, R. Lambert, D. Briggs, M. Gribbins, M. Spooner, B. Gribbins and E. Gibson. In the centre, from left to right: V. Briggs, S. Ashton, K. Ashton, -?-, -?-, M. Wragg and M. Ashton. Kneeling, from left to right: R. Spooner, I. Cheetham, G. Spooner and S. Gibson.

Fund raising has always been part of church life. Here we see the ladies of Bolsterstone dressed for 'The Old Village Wedding', posing on the Bolsterstone Vicarage lawn, c. 1921. Standing, from left to right: E. Haigh, H. Ramsden, Mrs Sanderson, M. Broadhead, Mrs Cheetham, -?-, Mrs Mason, A. Steel, Mrs Dyson, E. Haigh, A. Nichols, M. Ramsden and Mrs Broadhead. Seated, from left to right: Mrs Haigh, Mrs Ellison, G. Shaw, E. Sampson, I. Sampson, P. Dyson, Mrs Haigh, Mrs Farnie and Mrs Aspinall.

Each church had a choir, which would not only perform at the services, but, would often provide entertainment on other occasions. This is the West End Primitive Methodist Chapel Choir helping to celebrate the church's centenary, in 1966. Standing, from left to right: B. Henrath, H. Kay, with R. Crownshaw behind her, K. Jackson, E. Batty, P. Emmett, M. Harrison, V. Brookes, A. Bailey, R. Walton, E. Beck and B. Hill. Seated, from left to right: M. Watts, Mrs English, V. Hill, Mrs Gillott.

The girls of the Stocksbridge Congregational Sunday School pose for the camera. At the back, from left to right, are Dorothy Pearson, Dorothy Hughes and Gwyneth Sanderson. On the centre row, from left to right: -?-, Diana Hoyle, Christine Dyson, Jean Marston, Mary Hardy, Betty Marshall, Enid Peace, Cynthia Woodhead. On the front row, form left to right: Gwennie Butcher, Carol Castledine, -?-, -?-, Valda Knowles, Sylvia Crawshaw. (Photograph courtesy of Sheffield Library.)

Joyce Lindley was the St Matthias church Rose Queen of 1933. She is pictured here with all her attendants. From left to right: Violet Apps, Eileen Copley, Derek Scarriott, Myra Hoyle, Joyce Lindley, Mary Kippax, Brenda Tingle, Audrey Apps, Jean Walker, Margaret Luford and Brenda Askham.

Nine
Old School Ties

Most schools in the area had a maypole. The skill of dancing round the maypole would be demonstrated on occasions such as the crowning of the May Queen. Here we see the Midhope School maypole dancing team standing outside the old, tin school at Midhope, c. 1904. From left to right: Gussie Morris, -?-, Bernard Digweed, Doris Rodgers, -?-, -?-, -?-, -?-, Martha Roberts, -?-, -?-, -?-, Annie Taylor, Jessie Marsden, -?-, -?-. The teacher is Miss Brown.

Stocksbridge Church School was officially a National School. It was built in 1868 and served as a day school, Sunday school and church until St Matthias Church was built in 1890. On the back row, fifth from the left, is Fred Hollis. Harry Hollis is on the front row, second from the right.

A little further along Manchester Road was the Samuel Fox & Co. School, also seen in 1899. This building was later used as the co-op tea rooms, where wedding receptions could be held. This group of children from the infant class is showing off some of their apparatus and their inspirational pictures. On the back row, second from the left, is Nellie Bramwell.

We believe this to be an interior photograph of Stocksbridge Works School around the turn of the century. On the front row, second child from the right, is Vera Smith.

Stocksbridge National School later became known as Stocksbridge Church of England School. This photograph was taken c. 1930. Back row, from left to right: -?-, A. Lee, -?-, F. Holdsworth, S. Horton, A. Reynolds, D. Murrain, H. Staniforth, M. Walton, L. Crossley, I. Retallic. Second row (from the back), from left to right: P. Mate, N. Barlow, R. Broadhead, M. Shaw, D. Hall, F. Ellison, N. Whittaker, M. Turner. Third row, from left to right: J. Sutton, G. Hammerton, P. Elliot, M. Gaunt, W. Faulkner, M. Kippax, P. Carter, J. Hague, M. Hoyle, Z. Elliot, A. Stanley. Fourth row (from the back), from left to right: J. Whittaker, L. Pears, M. Brearley, J. Brearley, A. Couldwell, J. Retallic, D. Pickering, F. Brown, M. Clapham. Front, from left to right: N. Wragg, W. Armitage, E. Harley, C. Dyche, A. Ellison, S. Sykes.

Deepcar National School also became a Church of England school. This photograph was taken in the early 1920s. On the back row, sixth from the left, is Doris Rees.

If a child passed the County Minor Scholarship Examination, he or she would have the opportunity to attend Penistone Grammar School. These are the pupils in form 3A, in 1934. Several of these children came from Stocksbridge, Deepcar or Midhope. Back row, from left to right: C. Suggett, -?-, R. Whittaker, -?-, W. Hudson, -?-, D. Dowling, E. Grayson. Middle row, from left to right: J. Lindley, -?-, A. Kay, -?-, Miss Talbot, H. Chambler, B. Darwin, M. Hill, -?-. Front, from left to right: F. Gardner, -?-, -?-, M. Garner, M. Bancroft, J. Stafford, R. Butcher.

This photograph of pupils at Stocksbridge Church School covers two year groups. Back row, from left to right: B. Gosling, L. Webster, T. Copley, C. Clarkson, J. Rhodes, T. Bembrick and S. Mate. Centre row, from left to right: W. Houchin, R. Fletcher, A. Jones, R. Day, D. Hague, W. Beckett, R. Cook, E. Newbold, C. Bowskill and G. Carter. Front row, from left to right: Jennifer Charlesworth, R. Pickering, M. Withers, M. (or possibly C.) Robinson, R. Foster, V. Hoyle, C. Smith, M. Bainbridge.

When the county minor became the 11 plus, children from this area could no longer go to Penistone Grammar School before the age of 11. These children had to remain in a class at Stocksbridge Senior School in 1953, seemingly passing time, until old enough to take the exam. In the left hand row, from the back: M. Hush, -?-, H. Wright, S. Steward, P. Wood, G. Harrison, A. Hampshire, D. Hobert, N. Wragg and J. Newton. Right hand row, from the back: M. Firth, K. Stagg, S. Hemingway, D. Travis, J. Mills, A. Middleton and J. Oxspring.

Stocksbridge School opened in 1929, housing infant, junior and senior departments. The two wings shown were occupied by the seniors until the junior department grew to such a size that the hall on the far left, as well as the first classroom on this side of the hall, were required to accommodate them. There were 352 infants, 308 juniors and 267 seniors in 1930. Originally, the seniors came from Stocksbridge Works School, Midhope and Greenmoor. In 1938, pupils from Stocksbridge Church of England, Deepcar and Bolsterstone Schools also attended.

The staff of Stocksbridge Secondary School in 1951 gathered on the retirement of the headmaster, Mr P.M.W. Godward. He had worked at the school from 1930 to 1951. Standing, from left to right: R. Hinchliffe, T. Patterson, F. Sergeant, E. Creswick, Miss G. Carr, W. Thew, W. Briggs, C. Suggett and E. Hughes. Seated, from left to right: Miss G. Sykes, Miss B. Turner, Miss D. Pearce, Mr Godward, Miss E. Cree, Mrs M. Archer, Mrs L. Lawton.

Some five years later there had been a few changes among staff members. Standing, from left to right: F. Sergeant, T. Patterson, G. Gilbert, E. Creswick, T. Brown, C. Suggett and J. Frith. Seated, from left to right: Mrs M. Archer, Mrs M. Briggs, Miss D. Tyson, Miss B. Turner, Mr E. G. Balls (headmaster), W. Briggs, Miss G. Sykes, Mrs Addy and W. Dearnaley.

Here we see the staff who taught Stocksbridge juniors on the Shay House site in 1957. Standing, from left to right: Mrs J. Clarke, Miss J. Woodhead, J. Yates, E. Lines, J. Holland, Miss N. Pears and Miss D. Lindley. Seated, from left to right: Mrs H. Wiseman, Miss M. Firth, Miss M. Moran, R. West (headmaster), J. Auger, Miss S. Emmerson and Miss B. Rodgers.

We began this section with a photograph of the school maypole and we end it with the pageantry of the May Day celebrations. Here Stocksbridge infants celebrate in 1932. From left to right: Roy Saxby, Alan Aspinall, Eric Buckley (king), Jessie Kenworthy (queen), Nora Kaye and Walter Kaye.

The Stocksbridge Council School May Queen of 1936, Eva Elliot, was crowned by the Countess of Wharncliffe. The crown bearer, N. Tomlinson, and the train bearers, T. Castledine and P. Heath, were in white. The maids of honour, standing, from left to right: J. Ridal, J. Booth, E. Gibson, V. Wragg and kneeling, on the extrme left and right: S. Hanwell and B. Cox, were in green.

Ten
Brass Buttons

STONE LAYING BY F.S. SCOTT SMITH ESQ. WAR MEMORIAL

Although in 1919 a suggestion had been made to build a public hall to commemorate the end of First World War, it was finally decided to erect a clock tower in memory of the fallen. The foundation stone for the clock tower was laid on 14 July 1923. The ceremony was performed by F. S. Scott Smith, watched by local dignitaries and the Scout troop. It is hard to imagine how the money was raised considering the hardship in the valley at that time - 3,000 were out of work and soup kitchens operated during the six months coal stoppage in 1921. (Photograph courtesy of Sheffield Library.)

Armistice Day, 1924. This was the first memorial service to be held at the newly completed clock tower, which had taken less than 16 months to build. The gentleman in uniform walking down Nanny Hill is Clement Smith who served with the Royal Electrical and Mechanical Engineers.

Private Charles England (1898-1918) died while serving in the Durham Light Infantry, with the British Expeditionary Forces in Europe. Sadly, he was killed by a single piece of shrapnel that hit him in the head while he was in the forces canteen, behind the lines. He was awarded the British War and Victory medals posthumously.

Eric V. Heath, in his Royal Flying Corps
uniform. He tried to enlist while under age on
the outbreak of the First World War. He served
as an aircraft fitter from 1916 to 1918 but saw
no action. The only casualty suffered by his unit
was an airman who failed to avoid a propeller
that he was cranking by hand!

Another survivor of the First World War was
Fred Wood, seen here on his wedding day, 25
January 1919. His bride was Bathia Wragg and
they were married at Stocksbridge Church.

Women had to turn their hands to a great many activities during the war. Here we see the Stocksbridge Urban District Council Ladies Fire Brigade who served during the First World War. The male Fire Chief at that time was Ernest Jackson. Here we see his daughter, Dorothy, temporary Fire Chief, on parade with her crew, behind the council offices.

Stocksbridge Fire Brigade pose for the camera on Unsliven Road, in 1930. They are, back row, from left to right: A. Mussen, -?-, Evans, Chaffey (who was also a lamplighter), Tingle, -?-, Reuben Froggatt (chiropodist). Front row, from left to right: -?-, Crownshaw, Glen Charlesworth (Captain), Ted Holdsworth, Wilf Donkersley.

The same crew is pictured here. They have changed their hats for brass helmets and are demonstrating their skills with the hoses. Water was drawn up from the river through the large pipe leading to the back of the fire engine before being pumped through the hoses.

The same fire engine would appear to be still going strong in 1941. It is parked here in front of the fire station doors, in the yard of the council offices. Back row, from left to right: Pearce, Watkinson, Harold Haigh, Tingle, Clarence Fish, Norman Jennings, Harold Wright. Front row, from left to right: Tingle, Archie Mussen, Sam Berwick, Alvie Webster, Albert Jackson (greengrocer).

PC 'Bobby' George Jackson was attached to Deepcar police section from 1925 to 1938. He served as a sergeant in the King's Royal Rifle Corps during the First World War. He was wounded and gassed. In 1917 he was awarded the Military Medal for bravery in the field and in 1920 he received a British War Victory Medal. He also wears the St John's Ambulance Brigade badge on his sleeve.

The Stocksbridge and District Division of the St John's Ambulance Brigade can be seen here on duty at the rough-riding (motorbike scrambling) which took place each Sunday at Langsett between the wars. The attendant is possibly Mr Calton. The Stocksbridge Brigade was founded in 1908 with headquarters at Stocksbridge Works School. The superintendent was John C. Kenworthy and the honorary surgeon was Dr Mossman. First aid classes (for men only) were held at the works school.

1st Stocksbridge Company, Boys Brigade, c. 1909. W.H. Fox was the president. S. Blakey was the captain. The lieutenants were J.C. Kenworthy, W. Marshall and C. Threadgold. Dr Mossman served as the honorary surgeon. The brigade was open to boys aged between 12 and 17 and was non-sectarian, but the boys had to attend a Sunday school. Drill night was on Monday at the works school. The group is standing outside S. Fox's works offices. On the back row, extreme left, is Walt Swallow and second from the right is Bill Haywood. On the front row, second from the right, is Leonard Haywood.

No. 5 Platoon of the Home Guard is pictured here, outside the Central Research Department (now demolished) of S. Fox and Co., in 1941. Fred Harrison is on the extreme right of the back row and the photographer, Colin Castledine, is on the extreme left on the second row. Mr Castledine must have raced from behind the camera to appear on this picture!

Stocksbridge Congregational Girl Guides, c. 1944. Back row, from left to right: M. Hollins, C. Hance, C. Woodhead, E. Peace, -?-, B. Marshall, -?-, B. Thickett, -?- M. Micklethwaite. Centre, from left to right: N. Button, -?-, S. Crawshaw, O. Jones, J. Couldwell, M. Bacon, K. Tazzyman, -?-, B. Hance, S. Batterson, D. Hoyle. Front row, from left to right: -?-, A. Branston, S. Tomlinson, M. Peace, C. Bacon, Lieutenant D. Hance, Revd Sackett, Captain E. Newton, R. Walton, S. Walton, -?-, J. Garbut, H. Crawshaw, N. Tomlinson.

John Hull, seen here in his Royal Engineers dress uniform, and Marjorie Hull (née Hill) are pictured here, following their wedding which took place at St. James' church, Midhope on 6 July 1940. The reception was held at Midhope School. John served throughout the war and formed part of the relief force at Belsen Concentration Camp.

Eleven
Family Life

Our section on family life starts with this
delightful photograph of the Wragg sisters,
Florence Mary (who later married William
Lindley) and Laura May (whose wedding picture
features later in this section), at the turn of the
century. The smart dresses and high boots could
indicate a special day, such as Whitsuntide, or
perhaps a birthday with the doll's pram as the
main gift.

An Edwardian marriage, *c.* 1909. The bride and groom are Harriet Coultas and Percy Leather. Percy's brother, Joe, is at the back holding the child and his sister, Edith, is seated at the front with Madge Coultas. The housekeeper, who was known as Aunt Julia, is standing on the extreme left.

The Walton family, *c.* 1910. They lived in the Co-op Row at Deepcar. Back row, from left to right: Norah (who married Thompson Jagger on 26 Dec 1907), Ada, Beattie (who married Percy Schofield), George, Billy, Nellie (who married Daniel Webb), Ben and Evelyn (who married Jack Whitehead). Front row, from left to right: Mary (who married Fred Sanderson), George, Ellen, Reggie and Harry (who married Laura Keyworth, *c.*1908).

Another large local family was the Hanwell family who performed services as joiners, bakers and undertakers. John Hanwell, a master joiner, came from Denby and his wife, Sarah Jane, was born in Hunshelf. They are seen here with their children, *c.* 1910. Back row, from left to right: Dick, Helena, Willie, Minnie, Newton, Edith and Arthur. On the front row, from left to right: Mary (who married Fred Firth of Spink Hall), Jack, Tom and Gertrude (who married Tommy Hughes of Deepcar). The family lived at Haywood Park in 1891.

The changing styles of wedding finery can be seen on the following pages. Mr and Mrs Thomas Vardy are seen here, on their wedding day, *c.* 1912. Mr Vardy became the headmaster of the British School in 1924 and remained so until 1929 when it closed as a day school. (Photograph courtesy of Sheffield Library.)

On 18 June 1919, the marriage between Harry Hollins of Stocksbridge and Alice Couldwell of Deepcar took place at Bolsterstone church. Standing, from left to right: Ernest Couldwell, Fred Herbert Couldwell, Harry Hollins, Tom Wainwright and Joel Couldwell. Seated, from left to right: Elsie Smith (née Hammond), Alice Couldwell and Edith Wainwright (née Couldwell).

Here we see George Walton (seen previously with his family) with his new wife, Amelia Dorcas Marsden, after their wedding at Stocksbridge on 1 September 1919. Dorcas Marsden was a milliner and had a shop in Stocksbridge with a high reputation for fashion and quality. This probably accounts for the ornate and somewhat unusual nature of her wedding finery.

Posing outside Hut 30, Ewden Valley, after their wedding in Bolsterstone on 25 June 1927, are Eric Heath and Marian Hague. The bridesmaid was Margaret Hague, the bride's niece. According to a newspaper report of the time, the bride wore pale blue and the bridesmaid pink. The couple went to live at Shay Bungalow, Stocksbridge.

Remember the little girl with the smart pram at the beginning of this section? Well here she is again, this time on the occasion of her marriage to Joseph Walton, in 1929. Standing, from left to right: Leslie Schofield, Lillian Smith, Joseph Walton, Laura Wragg, Leslie Silburn and Edwin Wragg. Front row, from left to right: Mrs A. Walton, Kathleen Horsfield, Nora Hey, Phyllis Walton, Lillian Burrows and Mrs Sarah Wragg.

The bride and groom, seen here with their wedding party, are Mr and Mrs Hubert Roberts. They were married in Langsett on 9 August 1933. From left to right, they are: an uncle of the bride, Eva Portman, Ada Portman, Hubert Roberts, Phyllis Roberts, Percy Roberts.

The Hodgkinson family gathered here after the marriage of the eldest son, Charles Herbert Hodgkinson, to Hilda Cook of Deepcar. The marriage took place in Bolsterstone on 29 April 1939. Standing, from left to right: Barbara, Brian, Edward, Charles, Hilda, Kenneth, Leslie and Norman. Seated are Mr Herbert Hodgkinson and Mrs Hilda Hodgkinson. Kneeling, from left to right: Margaret Hilda, Alan and Jean.

Christmas is a time for family gatherings and here we see the Coultas and the Leather families partying in the mid-1930s. Back row, from left to right: Albert Coultas, Harry Ridal, Hilda Ridal, Norman Beaumont, Margaret Rusby, Louisa Coultas, Brian Coultas, -?-. Middle row, from left to right: Fred Leather, Mary Leather, -?-, Harriet Leather (née Coultas), Fred Coultas and Nanny Coultas. Front, from left to right: Dorothy Leather, Jean Ridal and Ella Beaumont.

The Leather girls are seen here in the late '40s, with their respective offspring. The ladies are, from left to right: Joan Herbert (holding her son David), Ella Beaumont, Margaret Rusby, Enid James (holding her daughter Linda), Dorothy Braddock, Mary Leather (née Gregg). The children, standing, from left to right: John Beaumont, Peggy Rusby, Pamela James and Jean Leather. Dorothy was the tailor for all the clothes worn by the family in this picture!

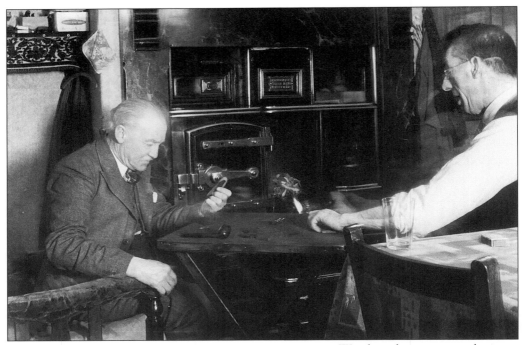

We close this section with two scenes of a more everyday, domestic nature. Mr and Mrs Gregg lived on Victoria Road. Here we see Mr Gregg playing a quiet game of dominoes in front of a Yorkshire range.

Meanwhile, Mrs Gregg is making the most of the sun by tackling the washing 'out back' with her mangle.

Twelve
On Stage

The young drummer, Joe Quinlan, stands outside
his home in Ford Lane, Stocksbridge, c. 1920.
However, Joe was not destined to play the drum
for a living. He actually found fame as the double
bass player with the Joe Loss Orchestra.
(Photograph courtesy of Sheffield Library.)

Another well known character in the district was Billy Birkhead, seen here in the centre of the front row. He organized and ran concert parties, this one from the First World War.

This is the Deepcar Drama Group, seen here in the late 1930s. Standing, from left to right: Blanche Booth, Harry Cook, David Charlesworth, Les Hudson, John Stanier and Nora Rhodes. Seated, from left to right: Vera Price, Freda Robinson, Frank Goodison and Doris Rees.

The Deepcar Pierrots, in the 1930s. Standing, from left to right: Geoffrey Dyson, Enid Dyson, Harry Hughes, Margaret Hanwell, Cyril Garwood (headmaster of Deepcar school), Brian Darnell, Nora Rhodes and Rita Firth. Seated, from left to right: Laurie Sykes, Percy Fieldsend, Adin Crossland, Freda Robinson and Joan Garwood.

The St Cecilia Choir, under the leadership of Dr W.M. Robertshaw, took part in many competitions across the country. This photograph was taken outside his house at Knoll Top, Stocksbridge, in 1932. Back row, from left to right: N. Moran, M. Mitchell, M. Couldwell, M. Cook, D. Leather, E. Stagg. Second row (from the back), from left to right: ? Broadhead, E. Briggs, M. Smith, L. Roebuck, M. Lindley, M. Challis, I. Broadhead, L. Hearsum, H. Nance, A. Wood, D. Broadhead, B. Rowbottom, B. Hayward, D. Rees. Third row (from the back), from left to right: M. Wood, E. Leather, T. Roebuck, H. Firth, B. Steers, I. Davies, E. Fieldsend, L. Firth, N. Staples, H. Cook, F. Marshall. Front, from left to right: E. Broadhead, F. Faulkner, D. Cheetham, E. Leather, F. Briggs, M. Battye, M. Dyson.

Here we see the members of the Stocksbridge Secondary Modern School orchestra, *c.* 1933. Included among the members were: Basil Marsden, the bassoon player seated third from the right, Kitty Booth, Gordon Waterhouse, Eric Sanderson, William Apps and Jack Copley.

The St Matthias Operetta. Middle row, from left to right: Ernest Wardle, Joyce Lindley, Mary Kippax, Eunice Staples, Myra Hoyle and Ronnie Davies. Seated, second from the left, is Audrey Apps and seated on the right is Kenneth Pears.

Most of the churches in this area possessed male voice choirs. Deepcar was no exception. Each year the choir would have a day's outing, singing and enjoying themselves wherever they went. We see the choir members here in July 1935 on a visit to Richmond Castle. Back row, from left to right: D. Truman, N. Allott, -?-, V. Dyson, H. Sanderson, C. Garwood (crouched down), -?-, J. Woodcock, B.Walton, -?-, -?-, -?-. Middle row, from left to right: W. Wood, C. Dodson, R. Hanwell, B. Digweed, T. Harris, H. Charlesworth, -?-. Front row, from left to right: J. Robinson, J. Challis, W. Askham, B. Sykes, B. Calton.

The area's most famous male voice choir is that of Bolsterstone, seen here in the late 1940s. Back row, from left to right: H. Hance, C. Crapper, R. Pearson, J. Gillott, W. Evans, W. Hague, A. Sampson, A. Firth, N. Hodgkinson, K. Hodgkinson, F. Copley, F. Jackson, A. Helliwell. Front row, from left to right: E. Firth, R. Davies, A. Portman, V. Hardisty, R. Thickett, T. Cooke, B. Hodgkinson, L. Creswick, J. Ellison.

The Stocksbridge Congregational Operatic Society performed several Gilbert and Sullivan comic operas during the early 1950s. *The Pirates of Penzance* was staged at the Victory Club in 1952. Back row, from left to right: Joe Hudson, Bernard Hill, Derek Shaw, Horace Hampshire, Peter Mortimer, Garth Jackson, Robert Hance, Rex Brearley, David Lines, Tom Birkhead, Eric Vardy, Jack Drabble, David Kellett, Winston Staniland, Colin Castledine, Michael Shore, Jim Shore and Neville Helliwell.

Middle row, from left to right: Nina Bramwell, R. Westwood, Nora Allott, Violet Richardson, Carol Castledine, Irene Cooper, Elaine Allen, June Marsh, Cynthia Bacon, Pamela Davey, Dorothy Bowden, Christina Cheetham, -?-, Una Dimelow, E. Hulley, -?-, Connie Longford. Front row, from left to right: Norma Tomlinson, Rhodison Revitt, Betty Hance, Fred Hill, Gwynneth Sanderson, Len Stoakes, Doris Barnett, Ernest Davies, Mary Revitt, Stanley Cook, J. Staniforth, W. Airey and Joan Digweed.

There has been a brass band in Stocksbridge for almost 150 years, the first one was formed in the 1850s. This is the Stocksbridge Old Brass Band of the 1950s. Standing, from left to right: J. Weywell, D. Musson, E. Dyson, P. Briggs, C. Mears, R. Firth, J. Sach, B. Lodge, G. Beverley, D. Godbehere, M. Wilson, F. Smith and C. Saunders. Seated, from left to right: Mr Durbery, M. Taylor, H. Taylor, K. Taylor, Ted Hodgkinson (vocalist).

The final band pictured is that of the Salvation Army, seen here in September 1970 on the occasion of their Golden Jubilee. Back row, from left to right: K. Broadhead, F. Hardman, S. Gibson and H. Noble. Seated, from left to right: M. Broadhead, H. Ellis, E. Gribbins, I. Cheetham, Captain T. Pheasey, Bandmaster G. Gibson, Mrs M. Pheasey, A. Broadhead, K. Shale, L. Cheetham, C. Broadhead, D. Hunt.

Thirteen
Jobs for the Boys-and the Girls!

Early industry in the valley, as in many other parts of the country, depended upon a good supply of water. The main rivers of the Don and Little Don, or Porter, fed by the numerous streams coming from the hills and moors nearby, provided the valley with an ample supply of soft water which could be used in a diverse range of industries. Armitage's waterwheel, on the River Don, was photographed by Denis Leather, in 1937. The water was fed along a goyt to Armitage's brick works.

This Biltcliffe photograph of Wortley Lower Forge, c. 1910, shows a busy scene. Its neighbour, Wortley Top Forge, is probably the oldest ironworks in Yorkshire. Both forges were known to be using water-driven hammers before 1650. While the Top Forge and its waterwheel have been preserved as part of an industrial museum, the Lower Forge has become a farmstead.

A mile along Old Mill Lane, Thurgoland, stood the Old Wire Mill. A modern stone proclaims its date of origin to be 1624 - this has been confirmed by records from the period. This is one of the earliest known steel-working locations in the district. The white patches, which can be seen on either side of the door, to the left of the building, are something of a mystery. It has been suggested that they could have been the result of the hot wire being drawn out and beaten here, the heat blanching the walls. Names associated with this mill are those of Jagger, Jubb and Stephenson.

This view shows Ewden Reservoir under construction at the turn of the century. Growing demands for water, for both industry and domestic use, meant that many of our valleys were chosen for damming. Work started on the adjacent Broomhead and Moorhall reservoirs in 1913 but was suspended during the First World War. The reservoirs were finally completed in the late 1920s. (Photograph courtesy of Sheffield Library.)

Local photographer, Mr Broadbent, captured this view of 'The Silent Weir' at Unsliven Bridge. Construction work on this reservoir was completed in 1905.

At the eastern end of Deepcar, in close proximity to the railway station, stood the brick works of John Grayson Lowood and Co. Ltd. The works were founded by Mr Lowood, Mr Reddish and Mr Gregory, between 1860 and 1870. Unlike many of the other industrialists in the valley, Mr Grayson was a local lad. He was the great-nephew of John Grayson of Spink Hall and he inherited a considerable amount of land in Stocksbridge and Deepcar.

This group of workers from John Grayson Lowood's is pictured at the turn of the century. The firm specialised in producing fire bricks for chimney and kiln linings, some of which can be seen in the foreground with the name Lowood stamped into them. Fire-stone clay was found locally and there were many day holes, or adits, dug into the hillsides nearby, following the narrow seams of gannister and coal that were required to make the bricks.

A pre-1900 view of Samuel Fox's steel works and Manchester Road, clearly shows how communities developed in close proximity to centres of employment. The buildings in the foreground are located at the top of Smithy Hill and the Coach and Horses Inn is seen in its original form. Both these buildings, along with the row of houses seen in the centre of the photograph, still exist today but many of the properties have been converted into business premises. The building standing on the right hand side of the road, in the distance, is the Work's School, provided by Samuel Fox. The two-storey building on the left is the British Hall, which originally, when it opened in 1828 as the Ebenezer Chapel, was a single storey building. (Photograph courtesy of Sheffield Library.)

This staff outing, of some of the employees of Samuel Fox, took place in July 1908. Dressed in their Sunday best, complete with caps and buttonholes, they pose by the Major Oak in Sherwood Forest. It seems to have been a men only outing. The two ladies present are probably the wives of two of the managers.

Hard at work, in the Tyre Mill of Samuel Fox & Co. Ltd, are William Helliwell (on the left) and Gus Withers. The steel tyres produced here were bought by various railway and tram companies, for use on their locomotives and rolling stock. This view shows blanks being forged using the steam hammer. The huge size of the machinery is evident, as are the hazardous conditions faced daily by the men. More difficult to imagine are the smell of hot metal, the noise of the hammer and the tremendous heat within the workshop.

Another view of the Tyre Mill interior, c. 1913, shows the tyres being put, and turned, in the block. In the foreground, from left to right: Reg Davies, Bob Sykes, Harold Senior and Mr Jackson. Local bandsman and singer, George Rees, composed a tune for a Christmas carol, which was transcribed for him by his friend J.B. Nichols of Bolsterstone. He named the tune *Tyre Mill* as he was working there at the time. It is still sung locally to this day.

The coke ovens were erected in 1916-17, near the Hawthorn Brook end of the works. They replaced the old gas making plant which used Halifax soft coal from S. Fox's colliery on Hunshelf. The plant purified and stored gas for the town. Coke was sold to blast-furnace plants, foundries and brewers. The Simon Carves 1917 tower was a familiar sight in the first part of this century. The plant closed in 1950 when the coal seam ran out. However, many locals will still remember the sight of hot coke being discharged from the ovens and quenched.

The coke ovens personnel, in 1929. Back row, from left to right: W. Winch, W. Watts, H. Clarke, P. Ryan, O. Watts, B. Gabbitas, B Bramhall, E. Wragg, A. Battye, O. Marriott, B. Mitchell, B. Wright, W. Mell. Centre, from left to right: C. Harrop, D. Blackburn, J. Wiltshire, C. Jackson, P. O'Brien, D. Hill. Front row, from left to right: J. Jones, G. Bellamy, G. Stamp, J. Hinchcliffe.

Samuel Fox & Co. were also well known for the production of umbrellas. The construction of the umbrellas was carried out by women, who were known locally as 'the umbrella girls'. We see them gathered here, in 1933. Back row, from left to right: H. Butcher (foreman), S. Hague, A. Padget, K. Brooks, G. Fletcher, I Boyt, N. Barlow, A. Wragg, E. Pears, B. Buckley, J. Woodward, O. Marsh, M. Tetley, M. Evans, O. Stanley, H. Evans, L. Hance, D. Yeomans, E. Johnson,

E. Clapham, E. Webb, M. Rodgers, I. Cunningham. Front row, from left to right: M. Kelly, I. Collery, A. Ranson, L. Goddard, B. Walton, K. Darnall, -?-, A. Worsley, Ms Shaw, B. Crawshaw, A. Worsley, -?-, P. Howard, N. Crofts, E. Sanderson, K. Steel, E. Bradwell, M. Finkill, E. Kilner, M. Harrison, M. Rodgers, I. Farrow, G. Woodcock, B. Sykes, I. Calton, P. Harvey, M. Burkinshaw, M. Jackson, G. Cardwell, I. Boothroyd.

The Little Don, or River Porter, runs adjacent to Samuel Fox's. The river was dammed to aid water extraction. This weir was part of the work's Dam Bank Reservoir and was known to have been in existence as early as 1880. (Photograph courtesy of Sheffield Library.)

Being adjacent to the river was convenient but not always safe. This view looking upstream alongside the Spring Mill, on 4 September 1931, illustrates that fact. After a period of prolonged heavy rain, the river finally broke its banks. One can imagine that 'The Silent Weir', featured earlier in this section, would not be quite so silent at this time!

Fourteen

The Customer Was Always Right

A. Marsden was a groceries and provisions trader located at 592 Manchester Road, in the Horner House area of Stocksbridge. The girl in the doorway is the Marsden's daughter. The sign in the window reads 'Closed Wednesdays', a practice which is continued today by many of the smaller shops in the valley. By the beginning of this century, a variety of businesses had been established in Deepcar and Stocksbridge, which were able to sustain most of the needs of the increasing population.

The cycle shop, belonging to G. Whittaker, was located near the bottom of Newton Avenue, in the Hawthorn Brook area. Presumably this is why the name for his locally made cycles was chosen. (Photograph courtesy of Sheffield Library.)

This advertisement for Whittaker's shop was found in a 1908 Stocksbridge Almanack. It illustrates just how versatile Mr Whittaker must have been.

Thickett's, the ladies and gentlemens tailor, located on Manchester Road near the bottom of Hole House Lane, is the nearest of the shops seen here. It opened in 1895 and remained in the family for one hundred years until its closure.

Next door to Thickett's shop was E. Noble's confectionery shop, seen here *c*. 1910.

This view of central Stocksbridge looks east from the Friendship Inn, *c.* 1930. The roads are bare of tarmac and horse-drawn vehicles still outnumber the motorised ones. The garage sign belonged to Knowles' funeral directors. They had started servicing motor vehicles in premises on Victoria Street. The car belonged to Mr Edwards, a school teacher.

A group of officials and branch managers from the Stocksbridge Cooperative Society posed for the camera, while on a visit to the Cooperative Wholesale Society factories at Lowestoft, on 16 September 1957. Back row, from left to right: J. Goodison, W. Wragg, D. Dearden. Middle row, from left to right: W. Carter, I. Stanniland, H. Clixby, L. Brookes. Front row, from left to right: J. Branston, A. Sweeney, A. Laycock, -?- (probably a representative from Lowestoft), V. Hardisty.

The Cooperative shop window display of 1937 was entered into a show and sell competition. The timing obviously coincided with the coronation of King George VI and Queen Elizabeth. Tinned fruit was on offer, with strawberries at one shilling and fourpence a tin.

Continuing eastwards we come to the centre of Stocksbridge. We can see the old post office run by J. Webb, with the Co-op chemist on the right and Marsden's chemist shop on the left. On the extreme left is Knowles' greengrocer's shop. The banner headlines proclaim, 'Russians routed, Japanese armies in pursuit'.

This photograph, entitled 'Proclamation, Edward VIII, Stocksbridge 1936', shows a crowd standing outside the butcher's shop of Charles Hague. This shop was directly opposite the Town Hall and the crowd is obviously waiting for the official proclamation, of Edward's succession to the throne, to be read from the Town Hall steps. The four councillors, on the left of the picture, are Luther Drabble, Vincent Challis, Percy Schofield and G.C. Knowles. The building to the right belonged to Mr Knowles and was used for motor sales and repairs.

The well loaded dray of E. and C. Jackson stands outside their shop in central Stocksbridge. According to the sign over their door, they were licensed to sell cigarettes and cigars. Their window poster declares them to be 'potato merchants' selling 'English and French Emperors'. Fry's products could be purchased as well as fruit, vegetables and Christmas wreathes! It is interesting to note that the adjacent house has a plaque over the door, which simply reads 'fireman'.

This full page advertisement of T. Bramwell, 'The Boot Man' was included in a 1908 edition of Hinchcliffe's Stocksbridge Almanack.

The above advertisement stated that Mr Bramwell had two shops. Here we see the branch shop, which was located to the east of the Wesleyan chapel at Old Haywoods, Deepcar, in 1907. The lady outside the shop is Mary Alice Sanderson. The children, from left to right, are A. Grace Bramwell (12 years old) with her two sisters, Ethel (aged 5) and Alice (aged seven).

DPC.3 MANCHESTER ROAD, DEEPCAR

Copyright Frith's

Old Haywoods, Deepcar, was an area noted for its thriving business community. Many of those businesses advertised in the Stocksbridge Almanacks, which were only published in 1908, 1909 and 1910. The Wesleyan chapel is just out of view on the left of the picture. The shop in the foreground will be known to many as that which belonged to Miss Ruby Wood.

This advertisement from a 1908 Stocksbridge Almanack shows the diversity typical of the small shops in the area at that time. Everything from gas mantles to cutlery and oil paintings to tea and coffee could apparently be purchased from Frank Faulkner's!

Still in the Old Haywoods area of Deepcar, we come to J.W. Revill the fruiterer. Many businesses touted their wares from the back of a dray such as this. It must have been a hard life for the ponies pulling the drays, with all the hills around the area.

Another diverse range of goods was to be found in N. Broadbent's shop, in Old Haywoods. One half of the double-fronted shop was devoted to stationery, the other was the boot and shoe department. Christmas is obviously close, the windows have been festooned with trimmings and a banner, wishing customers 'Compliments of the Season', can just be seen in the left window.

The Stocksbridge Band of Hope Industrial Cooperative Society made a lasting impression on the valley, one which is still in evidence today. Here we see the Deepcar branch with the name of Joseph Moxon over the door. He was the manager here until 1906. The premises were licensed to sell tobacco and patent medicines, also stocked was clothing, footwear, meat, groceries and general provisions. It is also known that this branch acted as agents for the Great Central Railway and tickets could be obtained in the shop.

This splendid photograph was taken outside the New Co-op Stores, which opened on 6 May 1910. The property became known as the Jubilee Building in commemoration of the founding of the Stocksbridge Cooperative, in 1860. The weather was obviously rather inclement if the umbrellas and overcoats are any indication, but there are still children to be seen in shirt-sleeves.

Fifteen
It's Only a Game

Stocksbridge is on the edge of extensive moorland, much of it privately owned, giving rise to scenes such as this, a grouse-shooting party at Hordren. After 1832, Game Laws gave land owners power over the game on their land instead of the Lord of the Manor. Bradfield Game Association was formed around this time and the local moors were kept well stocked with red grouse. For instance, 1913 was a great grouse year at Broomhead though the rest of the country had poor results. Its 4,500 acres of heather carried more grouse to the acre than any other moor in Great Britain. Standing behind the beaters, from left to right: John Hawksworth, Tom Beever and Ronald Beever. To the right are Exgrave Tom Fallas, Thomas Beever and Edward Armitage.

The Stocksbridge Old Cricket Team of 1897. Back row, from left to right: Jack Charlesworth, Fred Brown, Revd Easton (the local Wesleyan minister), George Emley (captain), Joshua Shaw, Paul Clixby, Willy Walker (secretary and scorer). Middle row, from left to right: William Heathcote, Jack Crossley, Joe Hoyle. Front row, from left to right: Fred Briggs, George Crossley, Frank Hoyle.

The Stocksbridge Church Cricket Club of 1920. They were the winners of division three, section A, of the Norton and district cricket league. Back row, from left to right: Bob Senior (umpire), Harry Butcher, Herbert Thickett, Marsh Swallow (president), Fred Knowles, Joe Pearson, Harry Button, Reg Sedgwick. Middle row, from left to right: Fred James, Frank Hoyle, Bob Sykes, Joe Wade and Charlie Pacey. Front row, on the left and right respectively: Sammy Apps and Frank Thickett.

Samuel Fox's general office cricket team, seen here, beat the laboratory team in the work's knockout final, in 1936. The score was laboratory team 24 and general office 30 for 3. Back row, from left to right: Harold Kippax, John Lemin, Ernest Smith, Arnold Grayson, Vin Jones. Front row, from left to right: Douglas Walton, Reg Jagger, Arnold Haigh, Harry Parkin, H. S. Forder, Ernest Goodison. (Photograph courtesy of Sheffield Library.)

The Stocksbridge Works Cricket Club, c. 1952. Back row, from left to right: W. Price, C. Suggett, T. Thomas, J. Brockbank, J. Faulkner, E. Beard, M. Ellis. Front row, from left to right: H. Denton, A. Burgin, R. Kippax, R. Burton, H. Rodgers, D. Dowling.

St Ann's Roman Catholic Church Football Team, *c.* 1920. Back row, from left to right: John Race, Father J.J. O'Shea (parish priest from 1918 to 1925), Mr Simpson, John Mann, James Marsh, John Kelly, Tommy Nagle, Vincent Marsden, Paddy Reilly. Front row, from left to right: E. Marsh, Joe Mann, Paddy Haley, Bob Tune, Michael Kelly, Alban Simpson.

Bolsterstone Football Club. They were the winners of the Penistone league in the 1928-29 season. Back row, from left to right: Roland Shaw, Stanley Chandler, Michael Kelly, Jack Smith, William Evans, Ernest Dawson, Charlie Coldwell. Front row, from left to right: Charlie Adams, Alf Brown, George Chandler, Willis Dawson, John Spencer.

Stocksbridge Council School Football Team, in 1929. Back row, from left to right: V. Whelan, ? Froggatt, E. Marsh, V. Firth. Centre row, from left to right: A. Shaw, A. Schofield, J. Thomlinson, ? Hardisty, G. Goodlad, Mr Vardy, T. Hoyle. Front row, left and right respectively, A. Spooner and R. Williams.

Samuel Fox & Co. Ltd Work's Football Team, 1938-39. Back row, from left to right: D. Beachill, -?-, A. Pearson, A. Heppenstall, S. Henderson. Middle row, from left to right: K. Wright, C. Suggett, E. Marsh, R. Butcher, W. Charlesworth, P. Dowling. Front row, from left to right: E. Webb, B. Henderson, B. Marshall, C. Dyson, F. Littlewood.

Stocksbridge Wheelers Cycling Club, in 1935. Back row, from left to right: Fred Harrison, Alan Green, Ken Tingle, Joe Milnes, Herbert Rodgers, Alf Day. Second row (from the back), from left to right: George Clapham, Jack Bradley, George Harwood, Harry Whittaker, Alan Walton, Harold Earsum, Fred Smith.

Third row (from the back), from left to right: George Godley, Gordon Walker, Ken Dyson. Front row, from left to right: Les Dimelow, George Torry, Norman Jackson, Verdon Hill, Reg Crossland, Ken Dancer, Maynard Broadhead.

Although team sports were popular, and tended to dominate the local sporting calendar, the valley had its share of individual sports too. There were two rifle clubs and a billiards room in the early years of the century. In addition most of the large employers had sports and social clubs. Here we see the gentlemen of the Deepcar Sports Committee, c. 1930, preparing to officiate at the annual field sports. Originally held in Lowood's playing field, it later transferred to the sports field at Bracken Moor. Second from the left on the back row is William Herbert, second from the left on the middle row is Raymond Rhodes.

Golf is another of the individual sports to be played in the valley. Here we see some of the Stocksbridge Golf Club members, c. 1950. From left to right: Peter Elson, Don Skinner, -?-, George Thompson (groundsman and club professional), Brian Langley, -?-, Fred Woodhead, Jack White, Colin Senior, Maurice Bell, Jack Burnett, Jim Hill, Stan Merry, Eric V. Heath, Vic Barlow, Harry Broadbent, Jim Copley.

STOCKSBRIDGE GOLF CLUB.

9th August, 1924.

DEAR SIR OR MADAM,

We are pleased to inform you that through the efforts of several enthusiastic supporters, we have been able to establish a Golf Course at Townend, Deepcar.

Rapid progress is being made in laying out the Course and same will be open for play by Members on the 30th inst.

The terms for becoming members of this Club are :—

(1.) Each playing member must be a Shareholder, the maximum being five £1, and the minimum one £1 Shares.

Where considered necessary the Management Committee will allow Share Capital to be paid by quarterly instalments payable in advance, but such Members have no voice in the affairs of the Club until fully paid up.

(2.) The Annual Subscription shall be £1 1s. for gentlemen, and 15/- for ladies, payable in advance in all cases.

(3.) No interest will be paid on Share Capital up to and including 31st March, 1925, and not more than 5% in any one year.

Sometime ago you agreed to support the formation of a Golf Club, and we now offer you the opportunity of becoming a member, and shall be glad if you consider the matter favourably if you will fill up the attached form of application, and forward with cash or cheque to Mr. F. Marston, 146, Oaks Avenue, Garden Village, Stocksbridge, not later than Monday the 18th instant.

It has been decided to make the financial year ending 31st of March in each year, and for this year have decided to accept a subscription of 10/6 for gentlemen and 7/6 for ladies, which is payable on application for Membership, and the full yearly subscription will then be due for payment on the 1st April, 1925.

Yours respectfully,

T. R. ABSON,	L. DRABBLE,
A. CAMPBELL,	W. HAYWARD,
J. KILBRIDE,	J. KNOWLES,
S. LEE,	ARTHUR SMITH,
ANDREW SMITH,	H. SAXBY,

Management Committee.

The founding of the Stocksbridge Golf Club and an invitation to join, dated 1924. Note the price of annual membership - £1 1s for men and 15/- for ladies!

To assure readers that we have sportswomen in our midst as well as sportsmen, we have included two girls teams. Here we see the Penistone Grammar School Girl's Tennis Team 1948-49. Those originating from Deepcar or Stocksbridge are, on the back right, Brenda Heath and, on the front row, from the left, Barbara Gaskell, Joan Charlesworth, and Peggy Rusby.

The Penistone Grammar School First XI Girl's Hockey Team, in 1950. Those originating from the Deepcar and Stocksbridge area are, back row, from left to right: -?-, Naomi Harris, Barbara Gaskell, Peggy Rusby, Marlene Mortimer, Valerie Goldthorpe. Front row, from left to right: -?-, Brenda Heath, Ruth Harris, Heather Armitage, Irene Morris. Heather Armitage went on to represent Great Britain as a sprinter in the 1952 Olympics.

Sixteen

Getting There

This locomotive, belonging to the Stocksbridge Railway Company, is believed to be the first one which ran on valley metals. It was supplied by builders Manning and Wardle on 12 January 1876, prior to the opening of the railway on 14 April 1877. The maker's locomotive number was 574. It had 12-inch diameter cylinders with 18-inch stroke and 36-inch wheels. The driver is William Williams and the gentleman with one hand is William Marshall, who was a Sunday school teacher at the Methodist chapel. Records suggest that the engine was disposed of in 1914.

Deepcar Station is shown here after being rebuilt in 1865. Looking towards Sheffield, the sign reading 'Deepcar for Stocksbridge' can be seen. The timetable of January 1846 refers to the station as Deep Car. In that year the early Manchester train would depart at 7.24am and reach its destination at 9.11am. A third-class single ticket could be purchased for three shillings and sixpence.

This is a view of Wortley Station, at the turn of the century, by Biltcliffe, a local photographer. The view looks towards Penistone. The original building was opened on 14 July 1845, but we see it here following its rebuilding, in 1888.

CHARLES ASKHAM,

CARRIER,

Manchester Road, STOCKSBRIDGE.

Begs to inform the inhabitants of Deepcar, Stocksbridge, and District, that

EVERY TUESDAY, THURSDAY and FRIDAY,

He will be prepared to carry

GOODS OR PARCELS TO OR FROM SHEFFIELD,

Leaving Stocksbridge at 8.30 a.m., and returning from The "Yellow Lion" Hotel, Old Haymarket, Sheffield, not later than 3 p.m.

PERCY C. MILLS

HAY, STRAW AND CORN DEALER, WAGGONETTE PROPRIETOR, ETC.

Large or Small Parties catered for.

Landau and Grey Horses supplied for Weddings or Private Parties.

Furniture Removed by Practical Men

With Spring Drays and Waterproof Covers.

CONTRACTING CARTER in all its branches

NOTE THE ADDRESS:

Henholmes, DEEPCAR, near Sheffield.

These two trade advertisements, which appeared in Stocksbridge Almanacks of 1908 to 1910, illustrate the carrying and carting facilities which were available in the district at that time.

The Stocksbridge to Sheffield bus service, *c.* 1915. The vehicle is an AEC (Albion Engineering Company) and is fitted with solid rubber tyres. This busy scene shows the typical fashions of the day, particularly the shorter skirts. The building is the work's school. The school has been extensively restructured over the years, but the roof line and gable end still remain.

The terminus of the Sheffield to Langsett omnibus route was here, outside the Waggon and Horses public house, Langsett, in 1924. The bus ran on Friday morning from Langsett to Stocksbridge market, where it would wait on Hole House Lane until the gas flares were extinguished at the end of evening trading before returning to Langsett. On Sunday, the buses ran as frequently as necessary to bring day trippers to Langsett from Sheffield.

This vehicle, seen here at Unsliven Bridge, looks brand-new. It was owned by Sampson and Mann of Stocksbridge. The vehicle was licensed to carry fourteen passengers.

Riding in style! A wedding party pose in a landaulet, c. 1920. They are pictured at the end of Bessemer Terrace, Horner House. (Photograph courtesy of Sheffield Library.)

The Stocksbridge Druids Juniors are seen here, preparing for their summer outing, on 27 August 1927. The vehicle was supplied by J.H. Gratton & Sons of Clarence Street, Sheffield and is parked opposite the Welfare Hall.

This charabanc, dated *c.* 1930, was owned by F. Bartlett of Stocksbridge and was licensed to carry eighteen passengers. The generously sized pneumatic tyres and more modern streamlining would have provided a much smoother ride than that given by the design of earlier vehicles. (Photograph courtesy of Sheffield Library.)

A ladies outing from the Friendship Hotel in 1930. The twenty-four passengers are obviously prepared for poor weather and ready for departure. (Photograph courtesy of Sheffield Library.)

A delivery van, c. 1935, is seen here at Green Farm with Mr Steward in attendance. This robust vehicle certainly looks as though it could cope with all the arduous work of travelling around the hills and valleys in the district. (Photograph courtesy of Sheffield Library.)

A view of Hayward's garage, Half Hall, in 1937. The man on the motorbike is Fred Harrison. The petrol at that time was 1s 3d per gallon - less than 2p a litre! Radio accumulators could also be recharged here.

Fred Harrison again, this time with Miss Muriel Crawshaw riding pillion. The cycle was a 1937 Levis, 500cc. The couple are seen here in 1938, two years before they were married.

Another fine example of a vintage motorcycle is seen here near the steelworks. The bike is a Vincent.

Here is a sample of what the weather can hold for our region. This is a scene on Boardhill in 1933. The snowfall caused the road to be blocked and the Dog and Partridge to be cut off for three weeks. The task of manually clearing the snow must have been arduous, but warm work, judging by the number of coats hanging on the fence!

Vehicles normally used for day to day working practices were transformed over night into colourful carnival floats, combining advertising with fund raising. Here we see the umbrella girls, on a work's lorry, in a charity carnival of 1925.

From a vehicle with horse power to a horse-powered vehicle! This decorated dray also took part in the 1925 charity carnival, possibly representing a primary school or Sunday school as there seem to be children only riding on the dray. In the background, on the left, are the railway sheds and, on the right, is Marshall's coal and coke merchants. The dray is standing at the bottom of Smithy Hill, which is where this book began, and thus our journey around Stocksbridge is complete.